JACK and the BEANSTALK

faith as a seed

Story Retold by BEVERLY CAPPS BURGESS

Illustrations by ELIZABETH LINDER

a faith tale

A Little Castle Book

Harrison House

All Scripture quotations are taken from
the *King James Version* of the Bible.

3rd Printing
Over 30,000 in Print

Jack and the Beanstalk
ISBN 0-89274-384-0
Copyright © 1985 by Beverly Capps Burgess
2205 W. Twin Oaks
Broken Arrow, Oklahoma 74011

Published by Harrison House, Inc.
P. O. Box 35035
Tulsa, Oklahoma 74153

JACK
and the
BEANSTALK

faith as a seed

a faith tale

ONCE UPON A TIME,
there was a little boy named Jack.
He lived with his poor, old mother
in a tiny, little shack.
The only thing they owned was a skinny cow
with a crook in her back.

Mother said to Jack, "The cupboard is now bare,
and even though I've prayed, it seems God doesn't care.
I guess when we get to heaven,
it will be much better up there."

Hosea 4:6
1 Peter 5:7

"Our cow is not worth much, Jack,
but sell her anyway.
Maybe you can get sixpence from someone in town today."
Jack felt terrible,
but he took the cow and went on his way.

Halfway to town, Jack met a happy old man
with a glowing smile on his face and a Bible in his hand.
He looked at Jack and said,
"Son, I'd like to buy that cow if I can."

Matthew 5:14,15

Jack smiled and replied,
"Yes, sir! What would you pay?

"Well, let's see . . .
I believe sixpence would be a fair price for her today.
And I would also give you my Bible
and these beans if I may!"

Jack looked rather surprised and said, "That would be fine!
I can hardly believe that the Bible and beans are all mine!"

The old man said, "Plant them, son,
and they will grow in time."

Matthew 5:16
Mark 4:26-28

"Read the Bible," the old man said,
"and you will find out how
to live in God's blessings
without having to sell your cow.
Faith is like a seed, and it must be planted now."

Jack ran home and told his mother
about the wonderful trade.
They laughed and rejoiced
about the money they had made.

But Jack kept thinking about
what the old man had to say . . .

John 6:63
Proverbs 4:20-22

That night while Jack was sleeping soundly
in his own little bed,
he dreamed of planting the beanseed
as the old man had said.
Then suddenly it began growing right up to heaven,
taking along Jack and his bed!

"Well," thought Jack, "maybe God can explain
what that man told me about living in God's blessings
and faith being like a seed."

Then a voice spoke boldly,
"Yes, Jack, I can help you indeed!"

Acts 2:17
1 Corinthians 2:9,10

God spoke to Jack again and said,
"All that I have belongs to you.
You need to learn what My Word says for you to do.
Then you will prosper and be in health as I *want* you to!

"Think on My words day and night,
then you will have good success.
You will find out I am not the one
who puts you to the test.
All I want is for My children to always have the best."

Luke 15:30
Joshua 1:8

"It's the devil," God said, "who steals, kills, and destroys.
But I have given you power over all the enemy's ploys.
To those who know the power in Jesus' name,
the devil's roaring is only noise!

"The devil has been devouring all My blessings
that were meant for you.
But you can plant your faith by speaking My words
like I created you to do,
and your seed of faith will produce a crop of blessings
made just for you.

John 10:10
1 Peter 5:8

"When My children are overflowing
with the good things that belong to Me,
they can reach out to others and set the captives free,
so that people everywhere will know
I am a God of love and mercy."

Jack said, "Oh, thank You, Lord,
for now I understand.
I am going to read my Bible as often as I can,
and I will be a doer of Your Word over and over again!"

Luke 4:18
James 1:22

God warned Jack, "I believe you will, My son,
but you must beware . . .
There is a roaming giant of unbelief down there.
Don't let him trick you into his snare."

"No, Sir, I won't," said Jack as he slid down through the sky
on a beanstalk that must have been two hundred miles high!

"I will remember what You said!"
yelled Jack as he waved goodbye.

Matthew 13:58
John 14:26

Jack awakened to his mother's voice,
"Get up, son, it's 8:15."

He slumped in his bed thinking,
"Oh, it was only a dream.
Surely I can't change things by the way
I talk and believe."

Mark 11:23

It was that huge old giant,
sneaking up on poor little Jack.

Then Jack remembered what God had said . . .
how the giant would attack.

So Jack yelled bravely,
"I believe God's Word! So, giant, you get back!"

Ephesians 6:10,11

That huge old giant ran away
as fast as he could.

Then Jack and his mother studied the Word as they should.

They found every promise in God's Word
that Jack had dreamed about.

And they lived happily ever after
serving God without a doubt.

John 8:31,32

And they never again lacked for any good thing!

*My God shall supply all your needs
according to His riches in glory by Christ Jesus.*
Philippians 4:19

Your New Birth Day

To accept Jesus as your Savior, pray this prayer now and believe it with your heart. Write your name and the date on the lines below.

Jesus,
I thank You for dying for me on the cross. I believe in my heart that God raised You from the dead and You are living today. Please come into my heart and be my Lord forever.

Amen.

_____ accepts Jesus as Lord _____, _____.
Name   Month   Day   Year

Sharing the Good News with Others

I remembered to share the Good News about Jesus with these friends:

_____   _____
Name   Date

_____   _____
Name   Date

_____   _____
Name   Date

"For my daughter, BreAnne,
who has sown so many seeds of love and joy in our lives."

Dear Friend,

As a believer and a responsible parent, it is so important for you to fill your child with God's Word. Our goal in this book is to engraft the Word of God into the child by applying the Word in a story that has been passed down for years. Your child will be able to see by example how to minister effectively and how to apply the Word in his or her own life.

The Scripture references on each page help you to relate the story and illustrations to the biblical principles you desire to develop in your child. Be faithful in reading and training your child in God's Word!

In Him,

Bill and Beverly Burgess

Scripture References

Page 4 — *My people are destroyed for lack of knowledge: because thou hast rejected knowledge, I will also reject thee, that thou shalt be no priest to me: seeing thou hast forgotten the law of thy God, I will also forget thy children.*

Hosea 4:6

Casting all your care upon him; for he careth for you.

1 Peter 5:7

Page 6 — *Ye are the light of the world. A city that is set on an hill cannot be hid. Neither do men light a candle, and put it under a bushel, but on a candlestick; and it giveth light unto all that are in the house.*

Matthew 5:14,15

Page 8 — *Let your light so shine before men, that they may see your good works and glorify your Father which is in heaven.*

Matthew 5:16

And he said, So is the kingdom of God, as if a man should cast seed into the ground; and should sleep, and rise night and day, and the seed should spring and grow up, he knoweth not how. For the earth bringeth forth fruit of herself; first the blade, then the ear, after that the full corn in the ear.

Mark 4:26-28

Page 10 — *It is the spirit that quickeneth; the flesh profiteth nothing: the words that I speak unto you, they are spirit, and they are life.*

John 6:63

My son, attend to my words; incline thine ear unto my sayings. Let them not depart from thine eyes; keep them in the midst of thine heart. For they are life unto those that find them, and health to all their flesh.

Proverbs 4:20-22

Page 12 — *And it shall come to pass in the last days, saith God, I will pour out of my Spirit upon all flesh: and your sons and your daughters shall prophesy, and your young men shall see visions, and your old men shall dream dreams.*

Acts 2:17

But as it is written, Eye hath not seen, nor ear heard, neither have entered into the heart of man, the things which God hath prepared for them that love him. But God hath revealed them unto us by his Spirit: for the Spirit searcheth all things, yea, the deep things of God.

1 Corinthians 2:9,10

Page 14 — *But as soon as this my son was come, which hath devoured thy living with harlots, thou hast killed for him the fatted calf.*

Luke 15:30

This book of the law shall not depart out of thy mouth; but thou shalt meditate therein day and night, that thou mayest observe to do according to all that is written therein: for then thou shalt make thy way prosperous, and then thou shalt have good success.

Joshua 1:8

Page 16 — *The thief cometh not, but for to steal, and to kill, and to destroy: I am come that they might have life, and that they might have it more abundantly.*

John 10:10

Be sober, be vigilant; because your adversary the devil, as a roaring lion, walketh about, seeking whom he may devour.

1 Peter 5:8

Page 18 — *The Spirit of the Lord is upon me, because he hath anointed me to preach the gospel to the poor; he hath sent me to heal the brokenhearted, to preach deliverance to the captives, and recovering of sight to the blind, to set at liberty them that are bruised.*

Luke 4:18

But be ye doers of the word, and not hearers only, deceiving your own selves.

James 1:22

Page 20 — *And he did not many mighty works there because of their unbelief.*

Matthew 13:58

But the Comforter, which is the Holy Ghost, whom the Father will send in my name, he shall teach you all things, and bring all things to your remembrance, whatsoever I have said unto you.

John 14:26

Page 22 — *For verily I say unto you, That whosoever shall say unto this mountain, Be thou removed, and be thou cast into the sea; and shall not doubt in his heart, but shall believe that those things which he saith shall come to pass; he shall have whatsoever he saith.*

Mark 11:23

Page 24 — *Finally, my brethren, be strong in the Lord, and in the power of his might. Put on the whole armour of God, that ye may be able to stand against the wiles of the devil.*

Ephesians 6:10,11

Page 26 — *Then said Jesus to those Jews which believed on him, If ye continue in my word, then are ye my disciples indeed; and ye shall know the truth, and the truth shall make you free.*

John 8:31,32